CW00392902

The HAUNTED COTSWOLDS

Tales of the supernatural in Gloucestershire

BOB MEREDITH

REARDON & SON
Cheltenham, England

Published
by
Reardon Publishing
56, Upper Norwood Street
Cheltenham, Glos, GL53 0DU.
www.reardon.co.uk

Copyright © 1990
REARDON & SON

2nd Edition © 1999
REARDON PUBLISHING

Written and Researched
by
Bob Meredith

ISBN 0 9508674 7 0

Cover Design and Illustrations
by
Peter T Reardon

Other Art work
by
Liz Yeo & Chris Burke

Printed
by
Stoate & Bishop (Printers) Ltd
Cheltenham

ACKNOWLEDGEMENTS

I am indebted to the army of people who have helped research this book, far too many to name individually. I would, however like to offer special thanks to Nick and Peter Reardon for their encouragement, understanding and support when things looked like going wrong. Also, a special thank you to Angie Rowlands and Peter Rollins of the Cheltenham Tourist Office for all of their help.
To everybody who has had anything to do with the preparation of this book.

THANK YOU!

BOB MEREDITH

I dedicate this book to the memory of the Late Wilf Cox. "Wherever you are, old friend, keep well."

INTRODUCTION

I am pleased to commend to you, the reader, "THE HAUNTED COTSWOLDS," second in a series of books containing Gloucestershire ghost stories. The first, 'Cheltenham, Town of Shadows', was well received and prompted further research. That book, in its turn, was successor to 'Haunted Cheltenham' which I compiled with the late Wilf Cox. Month by month, since the publication of Haunted Cheltenham, stories have been told to me by witnesses of unimpeachable character, so that when asked whether I believe in ghosts, my answer has to be, yes!

This in no way implies that I claim to know what they are, nor what causes them, nor why some people experience them and some do not. I leave the deep philosophical arguments about their nature to others, and confine myself to collecting the stories. I see myself as a folklorist, and hope my treatment of this book supports the role. My interest and appetite for the 'stories' knows few bounds. Indeed, had I lived two thousand years ago, I might have have been a Celtic storyteller.

Part of my thinking on the subject of ghosts is that people encounter the supernatural and then tell the story from within the framework of their own experience. The argument is safe in that it acknowledges the existence of forces beyond our understanding, yet appears logical. That is its weakness. Ever since the Renaissance we are driven to seek the logical.Scientific solutions to problems are praised and the existence of forces beyond scientific proof is denied. At the same time we are bombarded today by advertisements claiming quasi-scientific evidence in support of this product or that product. Little wonder that the exquisite thrill of mystery and fear of the unknown is weakening. Yet, it is not destroyed.

There still lingers, in those pockets of the mind where shadows are turned into demons and where things go bump in the night, a flutter of the heart when the clock strikes twelve and a yearning for firelit hearths where children listen to ghost stories on long, cold winter nights.

This is the true heritage of a people who existed before Rome brought its version of 'civilisation' to Britain and will continue long after the twentieth century is forgotten. The ghost story is not just a part of history. It is history!

AUGUSTINIAN MONKS & CHAVENAGE

A mile or two down a country road just off the A46 Nailsworth to Bath Road, stands Chavenage Manor. The original house dates from before the fourteenth century and almost certainly housed, at one time, members of the Augustinian priory sited at Horsley. This point could well be important as the tale unfolds.

During the sixteenth century the house changed hands a number of times until it came into the possession of Edward Stephens in 1564. At this time much extra building was done and the house was moulded into its current form. It is the Stephens family which furnish us with the first of several ghost stories attached to the house.

CHAVENAGE near TETBURY.   CHRIS BURKE 90.

During the time of the Civil War, Nathaniel Stephens became Parliamentary Member for Gloucestershire. He was related to Oliver Cromwell but was part of a moderate faction in parliament. His vote and support for the arrest, trial and punishment of Charles I was sought by Cromwell and Ireton. He eventually consented, and the rest, as they say, is history! Well, actually there was more.

Nathaniel's daughter, Abigail, was horrified at what her father had consented to and predicted a curse on the family. Sure enough, shortly after, he contracted a prolonged illness which was fatal. Now, the story has it, that as he finally lay dying, a spectral coach drew up outside the Manor. It was a magnificent thing, but was driven by a headless coachman. This coachman was dressed in Royal array and sported a Garter and wore a Star of the Garter on its breast. An unseen hand opened the coach door and at this moment, the ghost of Nathaniel Stephens came out of the house, dressed in its shroud, and climbed aboard. The whole ensemble moved away, but as it reached the Manor gates it disappeared in flames. It is further claimed that all Lords of the Manor who die in the house leave it in the same way.

Powerful stuff, indeed! So powerful that I paid Chavenage a visit recently and was entertained by the present owner, Colonel David Lowsley Williams. The house is even more enthralling than hinted at in the story. Straight away, as I entered, I was at the scene of some odd happenings concerning the family dogs. The Main Hall,

a magnificent room with a gallery, was once used by the family as the main living room. The dogs would frequently, while lying in front of the fire, become very restless and would look, in unison, at something which crossed the room from left to right. No one in the family saw anything, but that in itself was eerie. I was taken upstairs to the Cromwell Room. Around the walls hang seventeenth century tapestries, recently restored. A bed, on a Jacobean base, is covered with a nineteenth century patchwork quilt. This room was used by Cromwell when he visited the house on those fateful days when Nathaniel was pursuaded to vote for the impeachment of Charles I. The room was ice cold! I asked if the window was open and was assured it was not. The room was exorcised sometime in the past on the instigation of Colonel Lowsley Williams' grandmother, but not before a visitor to the house, occupying that room, had packed her bags in the middle of the night and had left, walking some seven miles to Kemble station. She wouldn't say what she had experienced; but, would you walk seven miles in the small hours of the night, for nothing?

Queen Anne's Room was the next on my itinerary. Here, Princess Marie-Louise, granddaughter of Queen Victoria, wrote some of her book 'My Memories of Six Reigns'. In that book she tells a story of her lady in waiting seeing a lady, dressed in grey clothes, but of the very finest, entering the Sir Hugh Cholmondley Room. Princess Marie-Louise was sleeping in that room at the time, and the figure bent over the bed, then rose and past out of the room again. When the lady-in-waiting mentioned the figure to her hosts she was told that it was "the lady in grey" and that she hadn't been seen for some time. This room sports another odd happening. The bed is made of very heavy wood and the legs are fastened by thick, long dowel joints. Two people are needed to lift the bed off the legs. A visitor to the house, on two separate occasions awoke in the middle of the night to find that the bed had been lifted off the legs and was precariously balanced. The visitor himself and alone could not have achieved this feat.

A third happening is attached to this room. While Princess Marie-Louise was using it she found that frequently the door would open without any obvious sign of human intervention, then would close again.

A room in the newer part of the house was my next stop. In this room some visitors were dismayed to find that they would be woken in the middle of the night by a swarthy man, dressed in uniform with heavy gold-braid epaulettes. This man had long, lank black hair and wore a long Mexican moustache. This room was also exorcised at the bidding of the grandmother of Colonel Lowsley Williams. In Colonel Stevens Room, an aunt of Colonel Lowsley Williams was woken on a number of occasions by something bumping into her bed. The bed was situated, at that time, in front of a door to the priest cell. As soon as the bed was moved out of the way of that door, the bumping stopped.

So, to the Augustinian monks.

In about 1067 a group of Augustinian Monks settled a priory at Horsley, very close to Chavenage. They did not, however survive the dissolution and Henry VIII gave their lands to the Seymour family. Many centuries later a chapel was built at Chavenage. On the surface of it, the two pieces of information are absolutely unconnected. However, some years ago a priest was invited, by the family, to stay at Chavenage to celebrate mass on Sunday morning - there is no official clergyman attached to the chapel. The priest arrived on Saturday and stayed overnight. On the Saturday evening he asked, at dinner, whether there was a monastery near amd was assured there was not. It seems that he had gone into the chapel to pray before dinner and had been astonished to see a monk, in a high cowl, bending in prayer at the alter rail. The monk did not move at the priest's entry, nor at his exit. Another visitor to Chavenage has also seen this monk walking in the grounds only to disappear near the chapel. The connection between the Augustinian Monks and this one makes very interesting speculation.

All in all, my visit was extremely interesting and I can recommend that Chavenage Manor is a must for all serious historians and ghost-hunters.

BURIAL MOUND STORIES

BELAS KNAP.

Burial mounds, of which there are seventy of the long barrow type on the Cotswolds, might be expected by some to be the centre of apparitions and odd happenings. Just outside Winchcombe there is Belas Knap, the world famous restored long barrow on the edge of Cleeve Common. This barrow, of the false entrance type, contained the remains of at least thirty-seven people.

BELAS KNAP from the SOUTH

One warm summer afternoon a family from the Midlands, visiting the mound decided to picnic on top of it - to enjoy the view. They laid a large table-cloth on the mound and loaded it well with food and crockery. The day was still and warm without a breath of air about. During the course of the meal the table-cloth suddenly leapt into the air, scattering food and the people.

The family were so upset by the incident that they quickly packed everything away and hurriedly left.

WEST TUMP.

West Tump Long Barrow lies in the woods off the Birdlip-Fostons Ash road at a point called The Buck's Head (Buck being a corruption of Boc meaning beech tree). The barrow, a great mouldering undergrowth-covered mound, though difficult to find, has its own atmosphere of fear at certain times. One Sunday afternoon a family visited the mound on a regular outing. The wife, well read and extremely knowledgeable of the pre-historic past, recently told me that during that visit she saw four neolithic warriors standing on top of the mound. She describes them as wearing leather, or maybe cream-coloured cloth, kilts and were naked from the waist up. They were bronzed in skin colour and held spears in their hands. Their hair was 'frizzy' in nature.

The barrow itself, of the side-chamber type, contained many male skeletons placed along the passageway to the south chamber and round the forecourt. On a semi-circular dais of stone within the chamber lay a skeleton of a woman and close to her the remains of an infant.

TAR BARROW HILL.

This interesting story from Cirencester concerns two men, at an unspecified date, who were digging for gravel at Tar Barrow Hill. The barrows, two round ones, can clearly be seen from the eastern by-pass. The men broke into an entrance passage at the end of which were several furnished rooms with statues and urns containing ashes. The furniture, when touched, crumbled to dust. In one room they saw the figure of a man in armour with a baton in his hand. The scene was lit by a light in a glass similar to a lamp. The figure suddenly struck at them, breaking their own light. On hearing a hollow groan they fled and the roof collapsed behind them, burying the contents of the mound.

NYMPSFIELD.

In the nineteen thirties an early Bronze Age round barrow, set on the scarp edge, fifty yards from the Nympsfield Long Barrow was excavated. It proved to be very interesting since it contained the remains of twenty-eight humans in a boat-shaped cist of drystone walling below the prehistoric surface. One of the people involved in the digging tells of a curious happening.

He was walking his dog near where the Round Barrow was being excavated. he climbed on to the barrow to inspect the pit which still contained the skeletons. The dog, being fussy and curious, jumped into the pit. Immediately, however it became rigid with fear and started to howl. This was something which he had never done before. Then the dog leapt out of the pit and ran off into a nearby wood, for he did not live far from the site. Two days passed before the dog returned home.

Some time later the bones were sent to the Royal College of Surgeons to be tested and dated. The man again walked his dog on the barrow. The dog again jumped into the pit, this time showing no trace of fear or distress.

BISHOP'S CLEEVE

A sound and business-like man from Bishop's Cleeve tells of an interesting incident which occurred while he and his family were taking Communion in a local church.

His wife and daughter were already kneeling at the alter rail while he and his son were standing waiting their turn. There were about fourteen people kneeling, with their backs to our informant, at the rail. As he looked at the backs of the people he noticed that one of the communicants was oddly dressed in a black, smock-like coat with a deep white collar. The coat was belted. The man also wore knee-breeches and black silk stockings. He had buckles on his shoes and looked like one of the Pilgrim Fathers. Our family man, waiting for communion thought that this communicant must belong to a special order of some sort. He thought no more about it until he turned to face the church and noticed the strangely dressed man had gone.

Later, on asking one of the sidesmen if anyone had left early after communion, was told that no one had. Oddly, the man's wife and family saw nothing unusual in anyone's dress that morning.

BREDON

My friend and colleague, the late Wilf Cox, collected this following account and I make a precis of his version of the story. Although Bredon is just over the Gloucestershire border into Worcestershire, it is worthwhile cataloguing the happenings concerning once derelict cottages. The former owner's wife helped convert the cottages and she gave a clear account to Wilf.

The first experience was that of footsteps walking across the floors of the upstairs rooms although one of the floors had been completely removed. The correspondent's sister stayed, sleeping in the third bedroom. She complained of an old man walking down the corridor who had woken her up. Once the floor had been replaced no more footsteps were heard.

The second experience concerned the sense of smell. During the years of conversion on the same date in November for two successive years, the lady telling the story experienced an exquisite perfume reminding her of massed flowers at a funeral. On the third year the doorway had been replaced by a window; the perfume never returned.

The third experience concerns a figure seen moving across the white wall of the cottage as viewed from the kitchen. To Wilf's correspondent, it appeared only as a vague shape which she expected but never saw go round to the front of the building.

The information is interesting and adds to the many cases where alterations to a building seem to disturb some presence inside.

BURFORD

Although Burford is just across the border in Oxfordshire it has strong links with the Cotswolds. The remains of the Priory is haunted by a little brown monk and the sound of a bell at 2 a.m. I spoke to a resident of Burford recently who confirmed that the monk exudes a feeling of deep sadness. The ghost which is seen in many parts of the Priory and its grounds, typically walks through walls and solid objects. The chanting of the monks is also heard close to the old burial ground of the Priory.

A house not far from the Priory has a poltergeist which screams, howls, moves objects and makes audible footsteps. Also, a man in old-fashioned clothes, carrying an old-fashioned gun is also occasionally seen in this house.

CAMBRIDGE

Some ten miles along the A38 from Gloucester lies the small village of Cambridge. The flat ground runs gently down to the River Severn leaving behind an old house situated on the Bristol Road.

This house was the scene, some while ago, of mysterious happenings. These all started, as do so many others, after alterations were done to the fabric of the house. The owner had lived in the house for over twenty six years without any sign of trouble. Yet, after these alterations the woman of the house began to feel the

presence of something by the side of the bed at night. Gradually the 'something' began to materialise into an elderly man wearing a trilby hat and a light coloured raincoat. Often the figure would appear on Saturday nights and on one occasion had an alsation dog with him.

Over a period of time the wife became accustomed to seeing the apparition and on one occasion reached out to try to touch him. This turned out to be a mistake. She found herself flung out of bed and was knocked unconscious for a short time when her head hit the central heating radiator. Her husband and daughter, of course, tended to her injuries but saw nothing. The husband, however did have something to add to the mystery.

He had heard what he took to be dice being thrown and music coming from downstairs.

CHELTENHAM

No book of local ghost stories would be complete without a section on Cheltenham itself. I add more stories to those collected in my previous book, 'Cheltenham, Town of Shadows'.

ARLE AREA

I visited one large house on the Arle side of town and discovered, not only a family home of immense character, but the setting for a collection of intriguing and unexplained events. Much of the activity seemed to be of the poltergeist kind. I was told about the sound of footsteps both upstairs and down and an occasion when the family heard the sound of footsteps entering the kitchen, but when they all turned to face the visitor found the kitchen empty. This also linked with the often heard sound of the latch on the kitchen door being opened. A member of the family said that at one time they had a relation staying with them and that what he saw turned him white. This relative, a sceptic, saw a door handle go down. The door was of glass and could easily be seen through; the relative could see nothing on the other side. Then, the door sprang open.

On another occasion the family heard a loud knocking on their front door. They opened it to discover no one waiting there. However, a police car was parked opposite, so they asked the policeman where the person had gone to who had knocked the door and he swore that there had been no one.

Name calling would also seem to be a common phenomenon. A member of the family might be at the top of the house and suddenly hear their name being called downstairs. At first they would go down to investigate only to find that no one had called.

Further occurrences involved a typewriter which was stuck in a cupboard at the top of the house and which mysteriously had the name of one family member typed on some paper around the roller. Also, when the beds had been made one morning the outline of a human shape could be clearly discerned in one of the quilts.

The Church of St Mary, Cheltenham.

When this is added to the occasions, many in number, when clocks and watches throughout the house have been altered, we have a collection of very odd happenings.

KEYNSHAM ROAD

A large house in Keynsham Road, now converted into flats, seems to harbour a lady dressed in black. A local businessman, solid in reputation and definitely not given to flights of fancy, tells of an occasion when he owned the house. He says that he was working late one evening and chanced to look around in time to see the figure of a lady standing at the top of the stairs. This figure turned and walked straight through a closed door. He saw her again on a number of occasions and describes her as being about thirty or forty years of age with a very pale face. She wears a long black dress. A tenant of one of the flats also reports seeing the apparition and describes her similarly, but adds that she was also wearing a white lace collar at the neck.

THE SUFFOLK ARMS

There have been some interesting haunted happenings occurring in The Suffolk Arms pub in town. There is a local rumour which says that the ghost is in consequence of a female servant who lived in the cellar when the place was a hotel. At any rate, the landlord tells of strange tapping noises in the cellar and objects going missing and mysteriously being moved.

Talk in the bar upstairs, following one of these incidents, leads to comments that it is the work of the Tapping Maid again. One of the bar staff refused to go into the cellar on her own after an incident when she was down there and heard a tapping noise coming from one of the other cellar rooms. She, thinking it was landlady, went to talk to her only to discover that no one was in the other room.

Well worth a visit for any interested ghost hunter!

SUFFOLK STREET

A correspondent lived in a large house in Suffolk Street for some years. While she lived there with her family they experienced an apparition on three occasions.

One morning when the mother was hoovering in the basement a girl appeared at the foot of the basement stairs. She wore a dark brown dress, just above ankle-length. There seemed to be another garment over the top of a lighter material which could well have been an apron. The girl had long dark hair which was tied back. She turned and walked through a blocked up doorway. The girl was seen on another occasion by the step-father of the family. This time she was sitting on the bottom step of the basement stairs and was in full view of a bright street-lamp. He thought that it was one of the daughters, but when he approached the figure it vanished. The third visitation was to a guest who saw the shoulders and head of the girl pass a serving hatch of a former kitchen on the ground floor.

The step-father also had an experience when he heard someone crying in one of the attic rooms. As soon as he entered the room it stopped.

CHURCHDOWN

In one of the older lanes in the village stands a bungalow built in the 1950's. This bungalow is the scene of an unusual story.

One day the owner was working inside the garage and was sitting on a stool. He eased himself away to reach a tool, but when he settled himself back found himself on the floor, because the stool had been moved a yard away. Nor was this the only odd happening. The owner has become somewhat depressed by constant knocking from inside one of the walls which continues for long periods of time. Within the bungalow objects disappear for varying lengths of time only to reappear in their original places.

The late Rev. Harry Cheales, exorcist to the See of Gloucester and former vicar of Wyck Rissington visited the bungalow and confirmed that it was occupied by a mischievous poltergeist.

CIRENCESTER

J.A.Brookes, in the book 'Ghosts and Witches of the Cotswolds', tells of the haunting of the Black Horse Inn. It would seem that some fifty five years or so ago a niece of the then landlord awoke one night to find her room bathed in a strange light. She heard a gentle rustling noise from one corner and when she looked there saw a spectre of an old lady, stout in figure, and bearing a nasty, unpleasant expression of face. This spectre floated slowly across the room. The niece was able, later to describe the old lady as wearing old-fashioned clothes made of what looked like long silk-like material of a fawn colour. She also wore a white apron and frilly mop cap. As the girl screamed the apparition walked through the wall. What remained was interesting; freshly scratched on a window pane was the word 'James'.

SPITAL GATE - CIRENCESTER. REARDON

A female medium was called in, who after assuming the identity of an old crippled woman declared that the trouble centred on one room and concerned an old man and woman. She also provided a formula based on the number three and white flowers for exorcising the ghost.

Another inn is troubled by ghostly activity. It would seem that over the years in this inn there have been reports about ghostly figures of monks and cavaliers. Cirencester, it must be remembered, was a Royalist Garrison town in the Civil War. At this inn poltergeist activity has been recorded such as the opening of doors, footsteps, moving objects and pressure applied to guests and staff, particularly in bed. A recent landlord reports seeing a dark figure in the basement part of the inn.

GLOUCESTER

GLOUCESTER GAOL

Reports of gaol hauntings are not common; oddly, one would assume since they have been the source of much unhappiness, suicides and often executions. Gloucester Gaol, however *does* have a story to tell.

The ghost of a woman can sometimes be seen in the prison. It is reputedly the ghost of one Jenny Godfrey, who was murdered by a drunk as long ago as the fifteenth century.

To this story can be added the comment that on one of the landings there have been many reports over the years of poltergeist activity.

GLOUCESTER CATHEDRAL from the NORTH-WEST

MILLBROOK STREET

A correspondent of mine tells an interesting story about a house in Millbrook Street. She and her brother were born and brought up in this house. Her parents were not well off when they were married and so had to stain the floors rather than put down carpet or linoleum. Her father didn't bother moving all the furniture, but rather stained around it. She says;

> "One night they were woken by a commotion in the room. They lay stiff as boards, too scared to get out of bed and put the light on. When it was all over they discovered the furniture had been moved and parts of the unstained floorboards had been exposed."

This was the beginning of the incidents, but was soon followed by other phenomena.

> "One night we had visitors. All of a sudden the cat went berserk and was spitting and clawing at something we couldn't see. Then it flew at the curtains and hung there still spitting. Someone opened the door and it ran out. The cat never came back into the house."

Other things included her mother thinking she had heard the brother come home, climb the stairs and slam his bedroom door, only to discover that he didn't come in until much later in the evening. Also, the correspondent reports feeling a touch on her shoulder and of something smoothing down the sheets while she was in bed.

WESTGATE STREET.

It is only to be expected that the city of Gloucester with its ancient history should have ghost stories to tell.

A recent series of events concerns a building in Westgate Street. A number of journals covered the story well, but a brief synopsis here might be useful.

Anglia Windows showroom was the scene of the trouble. It seems that poltergeist activity began to trouble the staff working in the building. The receptionist tells of footsteps being heard, lights which inexplicably flickered on and off, windows which opened mysteriously and a wardrobe which moved on its own accord. All of this was a precursor to a pool of water suddenly appearing in the window display where there was no water leak, neither from pipe nor ceiling.

A medium from Bath helped out in the end and reported seeing a stocky man wearing light coloured robes tied with a sash. It would appear, according to the medium, that this man committed suicide by jumping off the building. The medium's explanation to the events is that because the man shortened his own life he was trapped in the building where it had happened. It would now seem that the medium was successful in his task of helping the ghost to 'move' on.

Another old story of Westgate Street concerns a building, now pulled down, which while it stood was haunted by the ghost of a hooded monk.

STROUD ROAD

A correspondent from Gottingen in Germany provides us with this story. He was, at one time living in a large house in Stroud Road. The ground floor portion of the house was given over to a business while he occupied the upstairs section made into a flat; his landlord occupied the top floor. He says;

> "One Saturday night in September 1983 I was alone in my lodgings in Stroud Road, Gloucester, my landlord having gone away for the week-end. We lived in the two upper floors of a rather big house, the ground floor was a business. I was listening to one of my records and, when the first side was finished, I got up in order to turn it over. The music having stopped it was dead quiet in the house. But suddenly I heard a noise downstairs. It was a muffled sound, like an old person with slippers shuffling across the floor. Then it stopped, but could soon be heard again. This was repeated a couple of times, alogether lasting ten or fifteen minutes."

Naturally he was frightened and at first feared that burglars were responsible. He of course investigated and peeped downstairs but couldn't detect a single ray of light or any other sign of a burglar. Later he looked outside and inspected all the doors and windows, they were all locked. When his landlord returned he told him of the incident. His landlord took it all very calmly.

"I told him of the incident and he wasn't much surprised at the news. He even told me that once, while a friend of his was staying in the guest room on the second floor just opposite his bedroom, they both independently heard somebody descending the stairs in the night, each of them thinking that the other one had gone to the bathroom.".

PRESTBURY

In 'Cheltenham, Town of Shadows' I deliberately kept the section on Prestbury short. My treatment drew criticism from some readers who felt that the village deserved better at my hands. I will therefore attempt to make amends in this book. Prestbury has the age and history to command respect. With antiquity also comes tradition and folklore. The village of Pluckley, in Kent, at one time claimed the title of 'the most haunted village in Britain' with some twelve stories attached to it. I believe Prestbury warrants the title with over twenty tales. Historically, in late Norman times through to Early Medieval times the village had two large establishments - a moated manor and a bishop's hunting lodge. It was also on the route from Winchcombe to Gloucester which crossed Cleeve Common and dropped down into the valley via Mill Lane. This was the way the forces of both King and Parliament came to reach much disputed Gloucester.

(1)   I will begin the description of paranormal Prestbury with the story much loved by visitors and locals alike. The Black Abbot, by far and away the most well known ghost in the village, seems to cover a large area. The Abbot's wanderings occur, traditionally on three Church festivals in the year; Easter, Christmas and All Saints' Day. The walk begins in the Church. He then crosses the churchyard and makes for the grounds of the old Priory and from here enters the grounds of a cottage which stands on the main street. Here, he seems to disappear, apart from the times when he enters the cottage and is sometimes heard bumping around upstairs. His route varies on occasions when he has been seen walking in the direction of the Bishop's Palace, a moated enclosure which was probably the site of the Hunting lodge of the Bishops' of Hereford. Other witnesses have seen the figure in the High Street itself. A man of my acquaintance was forced to swerve violently while riding his motor cycle through Prestbury one evening when the figure appeared in the middle of the road. All in all the Black Abbot has become a

recognised local figure; a wit once suggested to me that the Black Abbot should stand for local council - I leave this as an interesting consideration.

(2)   A Medieval Messenger, a rider to Edward IV's camp at Tewkesbury in 1471, was shot, according to tradition, by a single archer. On Spring mornings the hoof beats can be heard and a faint phantom of a white horse and rider seen. I have recently spoken to a woman, living in Prestbury, who saw and heard this last year. Interestingly enough some years ago, during road works in the Shaw Green Lane area, a skeleton was found with an arrow between the ribs.

(3)   A cottage close to the Burgage boasts the ghost of Old Moses. One version of the story is that the apparition is of an old groom who occasionally drops into the cottage and announces himself when challenged as 'I'm Old Moses'. He seems to be harmless enough and, as far as I can gather, was last seen by several people in 1961.

(4)   Another Ghostly Rider is often heard in the Burgage and Shaw Green Lane area. This time the hoof beats stop suddenly. The story is that a Royal dispatch rider was galloping to Gloucester from Sudeley Castle when Prestbury was occupied by Roundheads. A rope was strung across the road, the rider brought down and immediately executed.

(4a)   A reported sighting of the horseman was made in the the early 1970's, but the place had moved to the junctions of Deep Street, Blacksmith's Lane and Bouncer's Lane. The apparition was both seen and heard - headless, mounted and was a vague misty outline.

(5)   The Burgage Area. A large house with parts dating back to the sixteenth and seventeenth century is host to an interesting ghost story. A horse is somtimes heard to clatter into the courtyard and stables, the rider then dismounts and enters the house. This horseman is quite distinct and separate from other Burgage horsemen. This same house has a room which is boarded up and not used. It is said that this room is haunted and a housekeeper in the 1950's told a carpenter who was working there that there were funny goings-on and noises in this room because her own was nearby. In the 1970's when alterations were being made to the building following a change of owner, two plumbers were putting a tank in that room. Our correspondent says;

> "They hadn't finished the job when they both came rushing down the stairs together with their tools saying that if their boss wanted them to work up there again they would hand in their notice. The next day when questioned about leaving the work unfinished they said that they had been busy fitting the water tank when they saw a figure of an old man dressed in white with a long white beard.

They were not so much scared by the apparition as by its unfriendly tone, as the old man was wielding a large, stout stick and he was shouting; 'Get out! Get out of here!'"

(6)   The Spinet Player. Another cottage near the Burgage has an enthralling ghost. The garden is haunted by a girl playing a spinet which has been seen and heard over the years. It would seem that the visual image has faded, but sometimes the spinet can still be heard. (Another version of the story is that it is the ghost of a music master playing.)

(7)   According to the 'Gloucestershire Echo' on Saturday March 4th 1989, Idsall House in Prestbury has a strange tale to tell. It would seem that a workman, while doing alterations in the house, now attractive offices belonging to the solicitors Bretherton and Price, was pushed from behind in the basement. He was on his own at the time! There would appear to be a hint of ghostly activity over the years for a member of a family who lived there once was afraid to go to the top of the house in case she met 'the apparition'.

(8)   A large house in the village, while used as a hostel for students, would appear to have been the scene of ghostly footsteps, inexplicable noises, doors opening and closing and lights being switched on and off.

(9)   A cottage in a short row in the middle of the village would appear, according to the present owner, to have strange lights shining there from time to time.

(10)   Mill Street [a]. The figure of a white lady has sometimes been seen crossing Mill Street and entering the churchyard. So far I have learnt no further details.

(11)   Mill Street [b] In 1982 a lad, with some friends, had walked some girls home to Prestbury one evening. The one lad, left behind for some five minutes by the others, walked down Mill Street alone. He had just turned a corner in the road, when a car approached him and in the headlights he saw the figure of a man dressed in a light mackintosh moving along the pavement close to him and going in the same direction. As he drew near, the figure seemed to weave and tack in front of him so much so that, being unable to pass the figure, he spoke to it. By this time he realised that no legs were showing under the three-quarter length coat. On being spoken to the figure turned and the lad could see that it had no face. It held up its hand and a light like a torch shone out from the palm. Then it turned away and immediately disappeared.

(12)   Mill Street [c]. A man, while walking his dog one foggy evening along Mill Street heard the sound of marching men approaching him through the fog from the

Shaw Green Lane area. The man's dog obviously in a state of terror sank back on its haunches, hackles raised. No men appeared out of the fog, but the sound abruptly stopped. A second witness I spoke to reported a similar occurence this time at the junction of Mill Street and Shaw Green Lane.

(13)   Mill Street [d]. The ghost of an old woman gathering sticks is still seen passing in front of the windows of a cottage in Mill Street. A path probably ran close to where the front of the cottage is now.

(14)   A house on the way through Prestbury, is claimed to be haunted by a strangler. The trouble is located in a bedroom where many who sleep there feel a sense of dread of being strangled. Tradition has it that a bride was strangled on her wedding night by a burglar who stole the wedding presents.

(15)   In the 'Source and Shopping Weekly' for Thursday 19th May, 1983, Florence Jackson of Prestbury mentions a leering monk seen in a house in Prestbury.

(16)   the Old Race Course. A lady and friend were returning to Charlton Kings late one summer afternoon from an expedition to Cleeve Hill. They intended to cross the Old Race Course and meet the road which would take them to Aggs Hill. Close to the gate of the Race Course they saw a man walking towards them. They thought that this was odd because as a rule no one walked on this particular path. When they reached the gate, however the man was not in sight. They both wondered where he had gone to, and thinking that he might have been a robber they searched thoroughly over the fence but found nothing. A little while later they met a clergyman and eventually they talked about the supernatural. They told him about the man they had seen and how he had vanished. The clergyman immediately told them that they had seen the Cleeve Hill Ghost and that he had heard a number of stories about this ghost.

(17)   In the same area as the previous story comes another, perhaps even stranger! A local teacher was returning by car to Cheltenham on a light summer evening. As she approached Prestbury from Southam she saw a funeral cortege crossing a field on the left side of the road. The party was complete with black horses, black-plumed and black-dressed mourners - a typical Victorian affair. Startled and somewhat puzzled she turned the car at the entrance to Noverton Lane and retraced her route, but the courtege had disappeared.

(18)   Bouncer's Lane. Several people have seen during the hours of darkness a glowing figure bending over as though working in the allotments off Bouncer's Lane.

(19)   High Street [a] On certain nights of the year, originating from an old house on the south side of Prestbury, the figure of a little old woman, dressed in

23

old-fashioned clothes, teeters along the High Street peeping in at the shop windows.

(20)   High Street [b] The proprietor of a shop in the High Street gives an account of a short period of what would appear to be poltergeist activity. Several nights in succession many items were taken from the small storeroom at the back of the shop and thrown in a heap in the middle of the shop floor. She also saw, on a number of occasions, a shadow moving across the room upstairs.

(21)   High Street [c] A large house in the middle of Prestbury is reputed to be haunted by a little old lady in a large hat who walks from the kitchen to the bedroom.

(22)   High Street [d] A singing ghost has been heard in a cottage in the High Street. The events would seem to have been common between the late fifties and early sixties, then heard no more.

(23)   High Street [e] During the 1970's four young women were walking westwards down Prestbury High Street after attending a women's meeting. On the pavement opposite the King's Arms they saw a man standing on the kerb waiting to cross the road. In the light of a street lamp they noticed that he was dressed as a jockey, with peaked cap, blouse and breeches. He started to cross the road but vanished before he reached the middle. Imagine their amazement when turning a slight corner they saw the same figure give a repeat performance.

(24)   High Street [f] A young man on a motor cycle turned the corner coming from Southam and Cleeve Hill when a woman dressed in long clothes and wearing a mob cap crossed the road. She walked up to two feet below the present surface of the road.

The young man braked so sharply that he was thrown off his machine and cut his leg.

PUESDOWN

My association with the Puesdown Inn, an ancient hostelry claiming roots as far back as 1236 A.D., is a long one. I first encountered the Inn while my dear friend and colleague, the late Wilf Cox, and I were out doing a spot of ghost-hunting. We had read odd snippets in various places about the reputed haunting at the site and decided to investigate. What we found was an 'Aladdin's Cave' of ghost material.

The Inn was a coaching stop for travellers on the old Saltway and was infamous for highwaymen. Its position, standing on the highest point on the A40, lent it a wild, lonely and bleak visage on the snowy morning that we first visited it. We were told immediately about 'odd' happenings at the Inn from the landlord and landlady. Knocking at the front door, we were told, kept people awake at night while bottles were constantly moved around in the cellar.

The traditional tale speaks of a highwayman called The Duke who, while working the road nearby, was shot. He made his way back to the Inn, hammered on the front door, but died as he got inside. Actually, another variation speaks of a poacher who was shot. A third version, possibly a hybrid, speaks of a highwayman shot by a gamekeeper. At any rate, the ghost of the person still knocks on the door of the Inn. The tale sounded like the sort of story that poems are made from; and Victorian melodramatic poems at that.

A short while later a new landlord took up residence and Wilf and I returned to ask some questions. Sure enough, the new encumbents also experienced knocking sounds on the front door. These were followed by footsteps crossing the lounge and then heard upstairs. These footsteps have, it seems, been witnessed by a bar full of people. Sometimes, when the Inn is closed and everything is quiet, sounds can be heard upstairs as if someone has got out of bed and walked down the corridor to the bathroom. This landlord also reports looking out of his bedroom window in the early hours of one morning to see the spectre of a coach and horses pull into his yard; complete with the sound of jingling harnesses.

Some time later another manager took over and I visited the Inn again. This time I recorded an interview with one of the staff and I include a transcript at this stage:

Interviewee: "Can you tell me more about the Inn than we already know? There's definitely a ghost here."

B.M.: "Tell me what you have experienced."

Interviewee: "The gas in the cellar has been turned off so many times...the microwaves in the kitchen...the bells keep 'dinging'...I came home one morning in the early hours, about two o'clock. I went into the kitchen and then I heard someone going into the bathroom, but didn't think much about it because the manageress was staying here also. In the morning she said that she had heard me go to the bathroom when I came in; I told her that I thought she had gone to the bathroom. This happens all of the time now.... One night the manageress was clearing a table in the lounge with her back to the stairs, she felt someone brush past her...the television keeps changing channels. Little things like this."

B.M.: "When we started you told me about some bedclothes being pulled off. What was that about?"

Interviewee: "Yes, now that was an Australian couple. They were in bed when he felt something pulling the clothes, his wife was fast asleep. On another occasion he went into the room and saw something. He yelled for his wife, but wouldn't say what he had seen. He wouldn't go into his bedroom again and he wouldn't speak about it. He's gone now."

B.M.: "Much of what you are telling me I have heard before from earlier landlords."

Interviewee: "I heard someone walking up those stairs last night."

The interview continued in the same way while other people added confirmatory comments in support of what was being said to me. All in all it was an interesting evening.

Some while after the managers changed and once again I visited the new person to keep 'tabs' on the situation. This time the manager claimed to have seen a person cross the one room late at night after the Inn was closed. Furthermore, odd wet patches began to appear on the upstairs carpet without any reason. And so the story continues. I will be interested to learn of further developments.

THE WELL KNOWN "FROG MILL INN" at SHIPTON OLIFFE in GLOUCESTERSHIRE   REARDON

SHIPTON OLIFFE

The Frogmill Inn stands back from the A40 alongside the road which the latter replaced which ran through the Shiptons, crosses the present A40 to Seven Springs, Crickley Hill and Gloucester. The Inn was probably the mill for the deserted medieval village of Shipton which was on the Andoversford side of the road and its mounds and hollows are still visible. Tradition has it that the building was a hunting lodge for the Black Prince (Edward, Prince of Wales) and if this is true it must date back to the fourteenth century and most probably earlier. In the year 1555 Bishops Latimer and Ridley were supposed to have spent the night there on their way to execution at Oxford. Certainly the Inn was on the old coaching road from London - Oxford - Gloucester and the post for Cheltenham in its early spa days was taken to and collected from the Inn.

According to reports from a landlord who kept the Inn from the late 1940's until the 1950's the place was much haunted and some of the manifestations have been notable. Recently the Inn has been extended and these additional buildings seem free from any apparitions. The wife of this landlord saw the ghost of her son, who had been killed abroad. This, almost simultaneously with his death. In the room used for entertaining travellers a kind of ectoplasm like a dense cloud or mist was observed, on occasions, issuing from each corner and meeting in the middle of the room. This was accompanied many times by whispering. A family having tea in this room heard the whispering of several voices. One young man who was working at pipelaying in the area visited the Inn for a drink one night. At closing time the landlady taking pity on the lad with such a long journey, in foul weather, offered him a bed in the room just mentioned. During the course of the night he was awakened by the presence of an old man, a young girl and a child who sat at the table in the room playing cards. Eventually he joined in the game, but the three suddenly vanished at dawn.

Numbers of staff over the years have told tales of slow plodding footsteps walking through the rooms used by the staff and two report seeing a figure crossing the bar in the early morning.

DELIGHTFUL COTSWOLD COTTAGES at STANTON, GLOS

REARDON

STANTON

A few years ago a colleague decided to take a friend out for a drive in the Cotswolds and finish up at a pub in the small village of Stanton. The day was fine and the drive had been pleasant so they decided to prolong the drive. They travelled over to Winchcombe and so to Stanton by that route. They turned off the main Stratford road up the Stanton road and had just gone over a small bridge when my colleague's friend said that she suddenly felt ill. Also she said that she felt as if water was creeping up her legs and that she was drowning; then her breathing became hard and she thought she was going to faint. My colleague suffered too. He said that a terrible feeling of panic over came him so the stopped the car. The feelings eventually subsided and they turned the car and drove home.

STOW ON THE WOLD

These occurences of 1963 to 1964 are reported in the 'Gloucestershire Echo' and the 'A.A. Book of Haunts and Hauntings'. The occupants of a semi-detached house, a couple and their young son, were amazed as pools of water began to appear in different parts of the house. A gush of water rose from the kitchen floor and streamed up the wall to the ceiling. Tapping, rasping sounds from cupboards and drawers, also the sounds of furniture moving, were experienced. The boy was thrown out of bed, sheets were ripped, a dressing gown flew off its hook and thrust itself under the mattress. Scratching noises came from the boy's bed and the headboard was gouged and scarred. A hand appeared from the end of the boy's bed and gradually changed through a childs, an adolescents and a mans hand. Writing also appeared on the walls of the house. By voice the ghost claimed that he was one of the builders of the house who had died on the date the haunting started.

So far this case has all the usual attributes of poltergeist activity, including water which is fairly common, but the next part of the occurrence is more unusual. When the family went on holiday they took the ghost with them to Devonshire. They became friendly with the local vicar and the ghost or poltergeist transferred itself to the church. When they returned home the house was free from haunting.

TEWKESBURY

Habitation at Tewkesbury dates back to Roman times and its religious settlement has its roots in the seventh century. Tradition tells that the first Christian establishment was built by St.Theoc, and yet another tradition records that the original monastery was built by two Mercian nobles called Oddo and Doddo and that this place was chosen as the burial place for Brihtric, a West Saxon king. Although the monastic order has gone, the fine abbey church remains. As one would expect, a settlement with such a long and distinguished history has many tales to tell and the ghost-hunter in Tewkesbury will not be disappointed.

The Abbey itself, as with many religious buildings, has its spectres. It seems that the figure of a monk can sometimes be seen leaving the west door of the Abbey before moving in the direction of the vicarage; details of this haunting are scarce. Another story tells of an old lady who regularly sees an apparition inside the Abbey.

Tewkesbury Abbey

A monk, dressed in black, emerges from a door, suspected of being an entrance to what might have been the dormitory to the ancient monastery, and silently glides down the aisle. On reaching the first pillar, seems to climb an invisible staircase before disappearing. Another story treats of ghostly moaning and screaming in the abbey heard by a local shopkeeper. Finally, the apparition of a white lady is sometimes seen in the churchyard.

The town itself is rich in legend and ghostly folklore, not only this, but has often been written about in literature. Dickens places Mr. Pickwick and his friends at the Hop Pole in Tewkesbury, while another Victorian novel, 'John Halifax, Gentleman' had its birth in Tewkesbury when the novelist, Mrs Craik visited Charlton Kings near Cheltenham, and travelled to Tewkesbury for a visit.

It is perhaps the Inns which command the lion's share of ghosts in Tewkesbury. One of the most venerable in the town, and dating back to the fourteenth century, is one such hostelry. Over the years odd things have happened at this Inn. One person who was brought up there in post war days recalls an incident where some horseshoes hanging on the wall of the bar suddenly flew across the room. This incident is interesting because it links with another haunting at the Inn. Many people record feeling the presence of something with an icy chill in the bar. A few regulars report seeing an old woman who sits in the corner without speaking and then suddenly disappears. One tradition places the spectre as that of a woman killed under the hooves of a carriage horse some hundred or so years ago. Maybe the horseshoes which flew across the bar are the very ones which killed the woman! Yet another tradition tells of the spectre of a headless man in chains which is sometimes seen at the Inn. Some years ago I led a number of parties of visitors to the Inn in search of this ghost. I didn't see it; but I did speak to a couple of regulars at the Inn who claimed to have witnessed the apparition of the old woman several times.

According to an article in the 'Gloucestershire Echo' during April 1985, a hotel in the town has a tradition of a 500 year old spectre. A soldier, it would seem, wounded during the Battle of Tewkesbury on Bloody Meadow, staggered to the Inn where he died in one of the vaulted bedrooms. He is, according to many guests and staff, still there in spirit. One past manager admitted that some staff wouldn't go near the room, but added that the ghost was part of the fabric of the Inn and didn't want it exorcised.

Another ancient Inn, dating from early centuries, also sports some haunting. On quiet winter evenings it has been possible to hear the unmistakeable sound of slow, plodding footsteps in the upastairs corridor. These stories date as far back as the late nineteenth century when visitors also remarked about hearing mysterious tapping noises. A more recent story concerns the wife of a past landlord in the nineteen sixties who, while walking along the corridor which hosts the footsteps, felt something brush past her, yet saw nothing. As with many ghost stories, details and frequency change. Some people experience things for a while and then the story gets lost and other traditions grow up.

Another hotel in the High Street, an attractive building, fits this category. I had gathered two stories about the hostelry from a source some years ago. On talking to the current manager of the hotel, was told that there was a bedroom which was not popular. The Manager knew nothing of the stories I had heard, but the room might be linked with the ghost of a woman in white who was once reputed to haunt the upstairs of the hotel. Some guests have experienced sleeplessness in this room, while other people have remained un-affected. This, of course, is the nature of the ghost story; some people experience things, others do not!

Two adjacent buildings in the High Street were the scene of poltergeist and spectral phenomenon some ten years ago. A friend of mine lived in a flat in one of the buildings and reports some very strange happenings. A number of times a selection of cosmetic bottles on a dressing table were arranged, untouched by human hand, into straight lines and then into circles and then back into straight lines. Marks, lines and blobs made with mascara appeared on the dressing table mirror. On one occasion on the floor above the flat a party was held. When the talk turned to ghosts a glass of sherry flew off the table and smashed against the wall.

The building next door had trouble for a long period of time. It had been used for several kinds of business. During the years objects have been heard moving about in the upstairs rooms and a lady in grey has often been seen going up the stairs. One day, in fact, a member of staff who, thinking she was a customer, called out to her that the public were not allowed up those stairs. When the lady reached the top of the stairs, instead of going through the door she went through the wall by the side of it. Of course an immediate search of the room discovered nothing.

A town clubhouse was the scene of some haunting during the nineteen seventies. A barman, while cleaning glasses in the empty premises, saw the figure of a man cross the room and pass through the door.

A local resident of Tewkesbury recalls experiencing poltergeist activity in Tewkesbury Park. This activity continued for a period of forty years!

BARTON STREET

Some years ago a man and wife lived in a building in Barton Street. One afternoon the wife was in the kitchen working when she heard heavy footsteps walking towards the toilet. She heard the sound of the toilet door open and close, and after a short while the toilet flush. She opened the kitchen door and looked out, but could see no one in the toilet or in the corridor leading to it. She now thought it must have been her husband, so went into the lounge to talk to him only to find him fast asleep.

VILLAGE LIFE

In a small village outside Cheltenham an odd thing happened some years ago. A young couple bought an old cottage about a mile outside the village. The cottage was in need of a good deal of repair but the couple immediately began to put it to rights. The cottage was very picturesque with a thatched roof and small windows overlooking the garden. It stood on rather a narrow lane, solidly flanked by tall thick hedges, unbroken except for the gate opening on to the cottage path. The cottage stood at right angles to the lane. The place had stood empty for some long while, but eventually it was in good shape so while her husband was away all day at his job she turned her attention to the garden. One mid-morning she chanced to look up and saw an old, short plump woman leaning over the garden gate looking at her. She had an old worn dress covered with a shawl and wore an old black bonnet. The young woman did not see the visitor arrive but that was not odd either for the gate was framed in the high hedge so that nothing could be seen on the lane beyond. Thinking the stranger to be a neighbour, the young woman greeted her and conversed about the weather, plants and gardening in general. The conversation continued for some time, then the young woman invited the stranger indoors for a cup of coffee, but the old woman politely refused saying she had things to do and moved on.

The young woman walked into the village to buy something to cook for her husband's tea. While she was in the shop she remembered the old woman and realized that she didn't even know her name or where she lived. She decided to ask the shopkeeper who seemed to know everybody. He could not place this old woman, however he called his wife from the back of the shop. At first the wife could not think who it could be but after a further detailed description including dress and mode of speech, she said;

"Why surely that's old Mrs. ----------- who used to live half a mile further up the lane from you, but it can't be, she's been dead for two years."

Undaunted the young woman looked out for the old woman the next morning. She kept looking at the gate but saw no one. She turned away for a second and the old woman appeared. A similar conversation took place. The old woman was natural enough. Surely the shopkeeper's wife had made a mistake! The invitation to coffee was refused again, but as soon as the old woman turned from the gate, the young woman hurled herself at the opening. The lane was empty. The old woman could only have gone a few steps. There was no other opening in the hedge.

WINCHCOMBE

Winchcombe remained, for many centuries, one of the most important towns in the medieval realm of Mercia. King Offa probably built a nunnery there in A.D.787, and there was also a royal palace belonging to the Hwiccian princes. Offa's successor, Kennulf founded an abbey there for Benedictine monks. This was reputedly dedicated to his son, Kenelm. The story of this dedication is interesting, although suspected of being a later fabrication.

> Apparently, Kenelm succeeded his father as king at the age of seven. He had an elder sister Cwoenthryth, who begrudged her younger brother his title and therefore schemed to have him murdered. The deed was done by the boy's tutor while on a hunting trip in a nearby wood. The young king was beheaded and his body buried under a thorn bush. Some time later Mass was being said in Rome by a Bishop when a bird dropped a piece of parchment. On it the bishop read a quotation from Chaucer concerning Kenelm. The details were sent to Winchcombe, and the monks found the body and bore it back to the town. When the sister heard of the event, she was filled with remorse, but not before her eyes fell out and her blood ran all over a book she had been reading. The beheaded body was buried in the abbey which was dedicated to Kenelm.

So sets the scene for Winchcombe's haunted traditions; and very interesting they are too!

The first story concerns a house near the centre of Winchcombe. Some years ago a colleague of mine stayed at the house to take care of the owners' dogs while they were away. The house was very pleasant and my colleague settled in well with his wife. After a while, however things started to go wrong and both my colleague and his wife began to feel that the house was resenting their presence. The atmosphere was very cold at times although the weather during that summer was warm.

Then the occurrences began. At first my colleague started to notice that when he and his wife returned to the house day or night, they found that the lights were on when they both knew that they had not left them on earlier. Also, one day they returned to find the radio on quite loudly when they knew that they had not put the radio on at all. Then one morning the wife of my colleague was frightened when the bedroom door knob rattled as if someone was trying to enter through a locked door. One evening the two of them were sitting in the lounge when the door was flung back on its hinges so hard that a piece of china fell off the mantlepiece. One lunchtime they were in the kitchen washing dishes when they felt something brush past them at the same time as it made a row of saucepans hanging up, sway from side to side. Also, they witnessed a bag of wool, kept downstairs, shake and move as they watched.

The main happening however occurred one night after they had gone to bed. The house had become really unpleasant so after they retired they locked the bedroom door. They went to bed but slept very fitfully. During the early hours of the morning my colleague awoke to find the taps in the bedroom sink gushing water. The dogs downstairs were barking furiously. Thinking that he had left the taps on, he got up and turned them off, then went to comfort the dogs. No sooner had he switched the light off however than the taps started to gush water again. This occurred throughout the night.

I spoke to the owner of the house some years ago and she confirmed that the house did have a ghostly tale to tell. This concerned the figure of a lady dressed in 'Florence Nightingale' fashion who had been seen often in the upper section of the house. It seems that neighbours also had seen this apparition at times.

A house on the opposite side of the town furnishes the second ghost story. This time it is quite an unpleasant one. A former occupant of the house tells of a ghost she encountered in the kitchen during the mid-sixties.

One evening the occupant was in the semi-basement kitchen when she became aware that a slight darkness was creeping over the room. Her first thought was that there had been a reduction in electricity for some reason, but after a few moments she saw there was definitely a shadow in one corner of the room. As she watched the shadow took shape until it was the form of an old woman. She was tall and had long white hair in plaits. The figure, according to the occupant, was so clear that she looked solid. Her face was thin and pockmarked and she wore a long white dress like an old-fashioned wedding dress made of lace. Behind the image the occupant of the house says that she could see an odd outline of some sort of trench which appeared to run right through the kitchen wall into the bank behind it. At the same time the room was filled with a repulsive odour of putrefaction accompanied by a feeling a utter sadness. After a short space of time the image became less clear until it finally disappeared.

Winchcombe, of course, has its very own ghostly monk. A friend of mine was walking home late one night down a small lane called 'The Monk's Walk' when he suddenly felt a breeze spring up and the air became very cold although it was warm and in the middle of summer. Then, from nowhere, a hooded figure appeared walking down the lane towards him. Again, I met a woman from Winchcombe recently who also confirmed that she had seen this monk.

THE WELL KNOWN "MILL HOUSE RESTAURANT"
IN THE COTSWOLD VILLAGE of WITHINGTON, GLOS

REARDON

The Mill Inn is reputed to have several ghosts. One of which is the spirit of a former landlady who drowned in the River Coln which flows through the village.

Some years ago a manager of the Mill Restaurant was almost driven mad by an intense and prolonged bout of poltergeist activity. Wine bottles flew out of their racks, saucepans and utensils were hurled off the walls and the place plunged into confusion. Other members of his family also witnessed these phenomena.

BIBLIOGRAPHY

PORTRAIT OF GLOUCESTERSHIRE'   T.A.RYDER
    Robert Hale.

'ARTHUR MEE'S GLOUCESTERSHIRE'   A.MEE
    Houghton

'GHOSTS AND WITCHES OF THE COTSWOLDS' J.BROOKES
    Jarrold

'HAUNTED CHELTENHAM'   COX & MEREDITH
    Glos.Library

GLOUCESTERSHIRE ECHO   various issues.

COTSWOLD LIFE   various issues.

'GHOSTS OF TODAY'   A.GREEN

'POLTERGEISTS OVER ENGLAND'   H.PRICE

'CHELTENHAM, TOWN OF SHADOWS'   MEREDITH
    Reardon & Son

LOOK _Out!_ for
our other products

Post Cards
Prints
Driveabout Packs
Post Card Packs
Cotswold Driveabout - Northern
Cotswold Driveabout - Southern
Calendars
and other drives and walks books

REARDON & SON
PUBLISHERS

56 Upper Norwood Street
Leckhampton
Cheltenham, Glos. GL53 0DU

Phone 231800
S.T.D. 01242